There's a Bully in the White House

Written and illustrated
by Colby Hopkins

Dedicated to all the people in the U.S. and around the world who are fighting in the struggle for dignity, justice, equality, and freedom.

There's a Bully in the White House
Colby Hopkins

The Humanness Project Press, New York
thehumannessproject.org

For requests for permissions or any other information, contact The Humanness Project Press at thehumannessproject@gmail.com.

ISBN: 978-0-9891086-2-1

Printed in the United States of America
Written and illustrated by Colby Hopkins
Cover design by Colby Hopkins

The Library of Congress has catalogued this paperback edition as: 2017918864

There's a Bully in the White House

Written and illustrated by Colby Hopkins

The Humanness Project Press
New York, New York

**THE HUMANNESS
PROJECT PRESS**

There's a bully in the White House. He's the biggest bully of them all.

But I'm not afraid of that big bully. I know he's actually really small.

I don't worry about that big bully, I'm not worried, not at all.

He's just like every other bully, and I know just how they fall.

Bullies have to pick on others, so they feel supreme.

They talk and talk and talk and talk, but never learn a thing.

They target other people, and call them hateful names.

They spread lies to demean, and to make them feel ashamed.

Now there's a bully in the White House, and that makes him unique.

But I'm not afraid of that big bully, because that big bully is really weak.

This bully insults women. He calls them nasty names. He treats them like they're objects, and dismisses any blame.

A person's body is their own, and no one has the right to touch it, but this big bully thinks he might, and no one can discuss it.

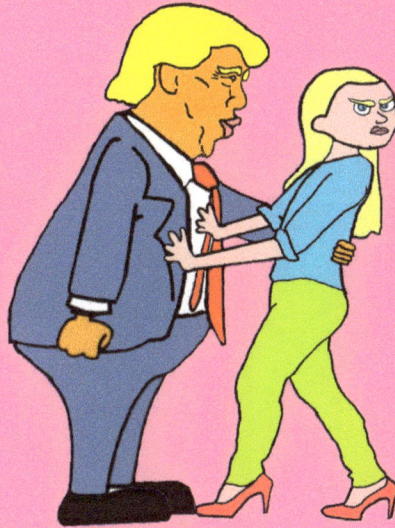

This big bully believes that women are not as good as men, but we all know that he is wrong, and his lies are going to end.

You see around the world, most women are fighting misogynists, so they would know a thing or two about how we should resist.

Women are so powerful, I know you will agree.

And when they stand together, they're as strong as strong can be.

And when they stand together, they fight for you and me.

Women are so powerful, they demand equality.

This bully insults Muslims. He calls them terrorists.

He wants the world to hate them too, while he shakes his little fist.

So don't let bullies fool you, they're acting out of hate. Bullies use individuals to blame an entire faith.

That bully wouldn't tell you that most people never hate.

It doesn't matter their religion, it doesn't matter race.

People are just people no matter where they're from, but that bully wouldn't tell, that bully's just too dumb.

Muslims follow Islam, as the religion they believe, and those who follow Allah are followers of peace.

They are all just people, like anyone you see, who want to live a happy life and raise a family.

But around the world, most Muslims are under constant threat, because these big bad bullies are as bad as bullies get.

But luckily Muslims have many, many friends. They stand with Sikhs, Hindus, and Jews. They stand with Christians.

And when these mighty Muslims lead folks of faith to fight the threat, we all join the struggle, because freedom we will get.

This bully targets Mexicans. He says that they love crime.

He hopes that most Americans will fear them all the time.

But most of us, we sort of know, our precious USA, has made the country Mexico a difficult place to stay.

And for everyone undocumented, the law is so unfair.
But we believe that everyone is always welcome here.

Like any loving neighbor, we'll treat our neighbors good.
We'll open up our borders, like every nation should.

We will help them do what's needed to find a better life.
And we will help make Mexico a country without strife.

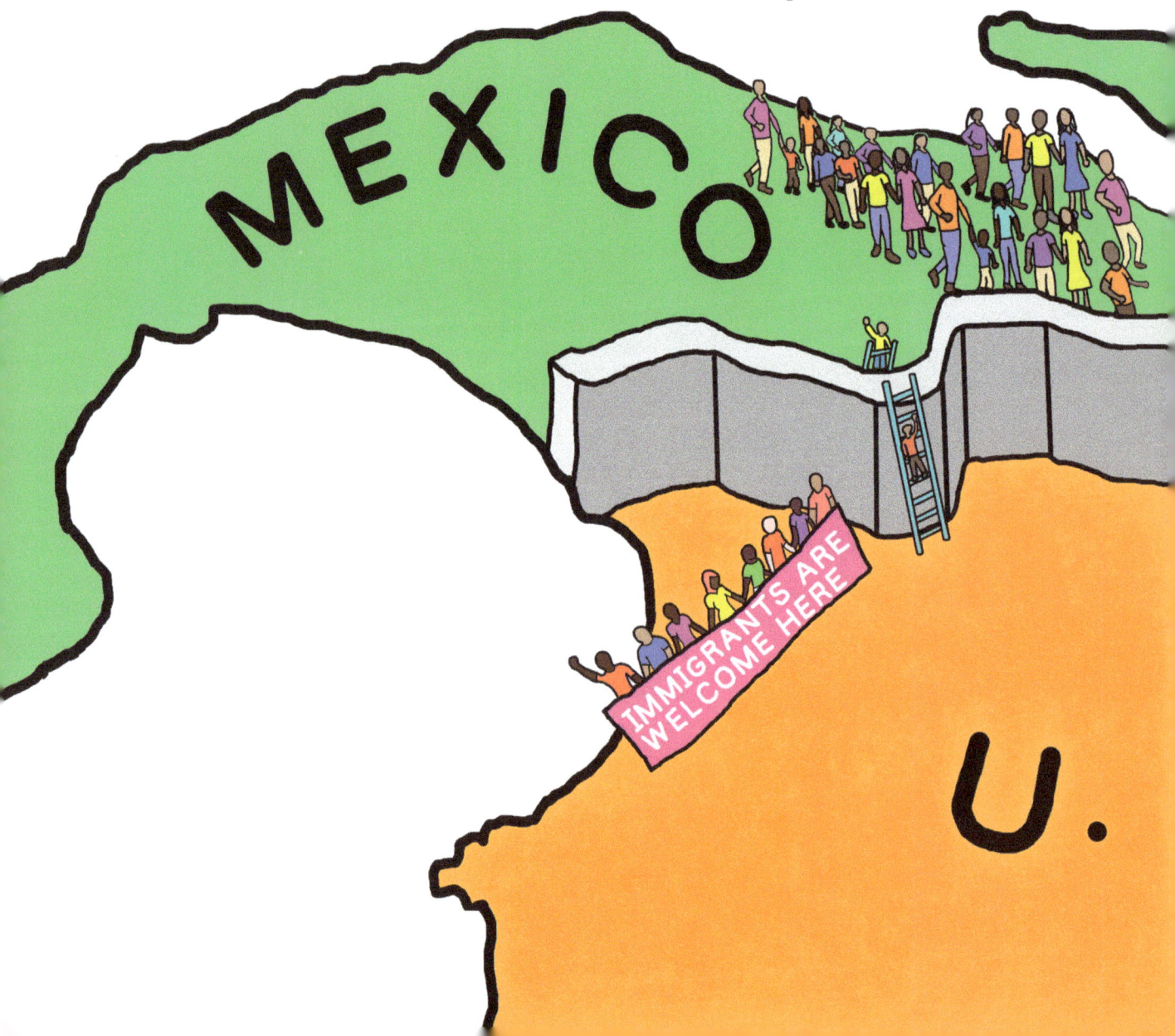

MEXICO

IMMIGRANTS ARE WELCOME HERE

U.

But while we wait for better days, this country is for all. So we won't let that big bad bully build his stupid wall.

Mexicans have joined us here and make this country great. They're fighting for their families with love and hope and faith.

So bold and courageous, they fight for you and me. With great determination, they fight for dignity.

S.A.

This bully insults Black people. They are thugs is what he claims.

He's promoting so much racism, he should really be ashamed.

This big ol' bully drums up fear. It really is a pity.

He's scaring all these white folks now, demonizing inner cities.

But we all know about these lies and U.S. history.

Black people have overcome so much pain and so much misery.

That is why they know just how to make big bullies scatter.

They persevere and they will fight, and make sure Black Lives Matter.

Brave and persistent, Black folks abolish unjust power and white supremacy.

They fight with love and wisdom, and they build community.

They've been fighting for so long. They'll keep fighting, you can trust this.

They lead the struggle for what's right, you see, they fight for justice.

Now there's a bully in the White House. He likes to think he's king.

But we will show that bully exactly what we think.

This bully is a coward. He is weak, and insecure.

He might be a grown-up, but he's always immature.

So there's a bully in the White House. He's the biggest bully of them all.

But I am not afraid of that big bully, I know he's just really small.

This bully's mocking people with disabilities.

He pretends that they are weaklings, and hopes
everyone agrees.

This bully slanders immigrants and targets refugees.

Like all the other bullies, he attacks anyone in need.

He attacks feminists, socialists, activists, and anyone who disagrees.

He will target everyone who is fighting to be free.

He discredits journalists, who challenge his authority.

He tries to bully everyone and dominate the story.

He attacks all people who are LGBTQI.

He will attack anyone and spread his vicious lies.

He needs to be a bully to get other bullies to support, but there are more of us than them, I'm happy to report.

We are people who understand that every human being, who walks the earth deserves to live with their dignity.

We understand that everyone who's living, should live free.

We can love who we wish, and be treated equally.

We will have our justice, and then there will be peace.

We will govern ourselves now, and bring corrupt power to its knees.

We are those that understand that none of us is free, until the day we have a say in our society.

We are those that understand that we must win the struggle.

Power to the people ya'll, all bullies are in trouble.

Freedom, equality, justice, and dignity, these are our demands.

Bullies cannot stop us. The people rule this land.

America may have its flaws, but we will make it free.

We will not be bullied by a bully. This is our democracy.

We will vote, we will boycott, we will organize.

We will build our own communities, and together we will rise.

We will fight all oppressors, colonizers, and imperialists.

We will take back all that is ours. We will fight and we'll resist.

If a big bad bully attacks just one, then that bully attacks us all.

I'm not afraid of that big bully, because I am standing with you all.

For a glossary of terms, discussion guide, and other resources to use with children regarding *There's a Bully in the White House*, please visit thehumannessproject.org.

www.ingramcontent.com/pod-product-compliance
Lightning Source LLC
Chambersburg PA
CBHW041610260326

41914CB00012B/1450